Ella Bop
A Coloring Book For Pregnant Ladies

© 2012 Ella Bop
Outside The Lines Press

ISBN-13: 978-0-615-72976-3

www.outsidethelinespress.com

ALL RIGHTS RESERVED.

This book contains material protected under International and Federal Copyright Laws and Treaties. Any unauthorized reprint or use of this material is prohibited. No part of this book may be reproduced or transmitted in any form or by any means, electronic or mechanical, including photocopying, recording, or by any information storage and retrieval system without express written permission from the author / publisher.

Severe morning sickness affects 5 out of 6 pregnant women

Eating habits can be significantly altered by the energy demands of pregnancy

"I'm sorry, did you say eight cheeseburgers?"

"Don't judge me!"

Help the pregnant lady find her pickles

Modern diagnostic equipment makes it possible to view crystal clear images of your baby in utero

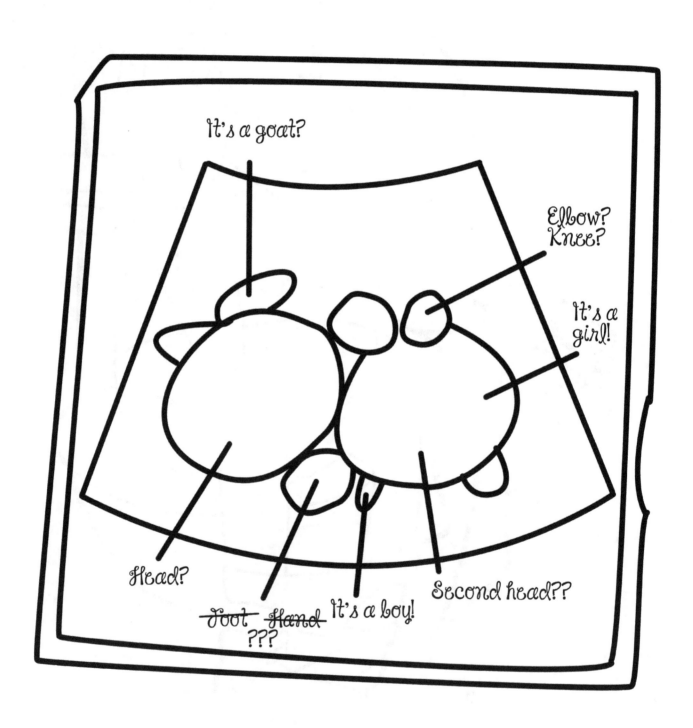

Pregnant Lady Word Find

```
T S S T M L K Q S S O L L I H V
B S T P Z E H C A K C A B N L X
G B R E E C H T L P I T O C I N
F I E S U S N D Q Y E R T O Z R
O O S N I E V R E D I P S N T N
N X S G C I D M E E P S B T E H
S Y R A K C Y M O T O I S I P E
E E L U J I A E E D U J C N I S
E P D V L C E C Z O H Y N E D U
E I T C C S O O T P E X Z N U T
R E O I O M F N T D Y L T C R N
L P U P E S W I G P B E R E A E
E V F H I V E U R N A Q M S L D
O S T E C R T M T F E S P E S D
C E F E G S Q L N T E A O E T K
Q N I Y U C P O A E A A A E R O
```

stress
incontinence
spider veins
breech
pitocin
episiotomy

placenta
meconium
backache
edema
epidural

Prenatal yoga is ideal for keeping healthy and happy throughout your pregnancy

"Hello, fire department? I'm going to need assistance..."

The urge to touch a pregnant lady's belly is almost irresistible.

"Rub *his* belly! It's bigger than mine!"

Pregnant women share a special bond

"If you're not going to eat your placenta, can I have it?"

Swelling of the feet and hands is common during pregnancy

"Honey, I don't want to alarm you, but your ankles seem to have eaten your toes."

When you're pregnant, suddenly everyone's a medical expert.

"Did you know that if you sleep on your left side it will increase blood flow to the placenta?"

Modern maternity clothing is both fashionable and practical

"Whatever! I'm comfortable."

Cut out the below ingredients and design your own craving-sandwich with wildly inappropriate food combinations

You can often recognize a pregnant lady by her radiant glow

"Pregnancy acne? Are you kidding me??"

Match the picture of the popular birthing location with its title

Back seat of a 2008 Toyota Camry

CABC Accredited Women's Health and Birth Center

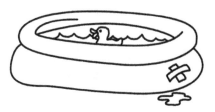

Second hand home birthing pool bought on eBay for $279

The closest hospital

Some questions are more welcome than others

"You're so big! Are you having twins?"

"Come stand a little closer and ask that again."

The growing fetus often places considerable pressure on the bladder

"Oh my god, did your water just break?" "No, I just peed myself a little. No worries."

First time mothers are filled with great intentions

"I'm hoping to have him toilet trained by the time he's 6 months."

"Good luck with that."

Changes to the family budget might be necessary to accommodate the added expense of having a newborn

False labor is common throughout the third trimester

"Don't worry honey, it's just Toni Braxton Hicks contractions"

Help the semi-hysterical husband find the quickest route to the hospital

Childbirth is one of the most rewarding experiences in a woman's life

"What do you mean losing bowel control is 'perfectly normal'??"

During labor, everyone's obsessed with your cervix

"As you can see, she is fully dilated."

Uh-oh, the baby's stuck in the birth canal! Connect the dots to find out what the OB GYN will use to extract him.

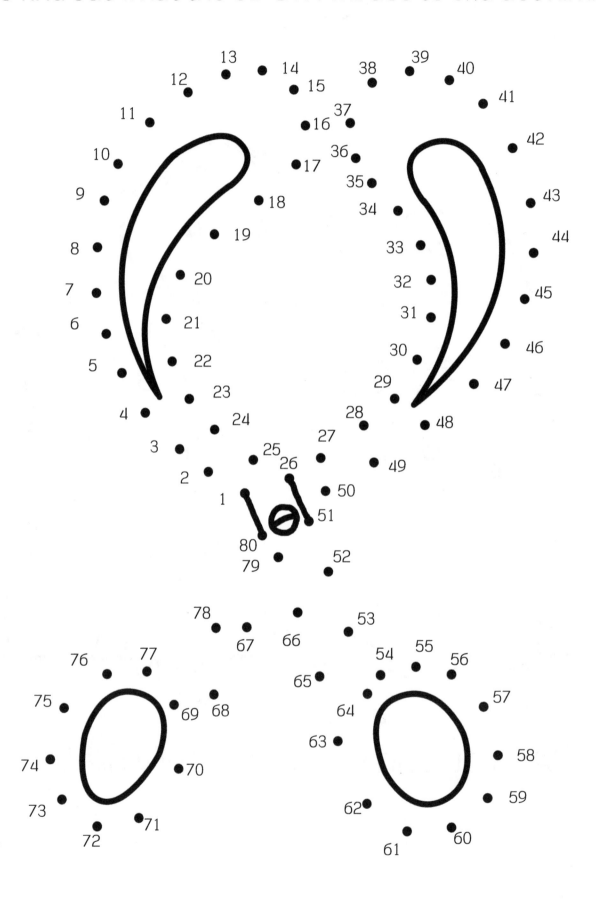

A new father savors the moment

"I can't unsee that. Oh god, I can't unsee that!"

Totally worth it

For more from the series *Ironic Coloring Books for Adults* from Outside The Lines Press, visit:

www.outsidethelinespress.com

Coming soon:

A Coloring Book for Brides
A Coloring Book for Bridesmaids
A Coloring Book for Newlyweds
A Coloring Book for New Parents
A Coloring Book for Dog Lovers
A Coloring Book for Cat Lovers
A Coloring Book for 30 Somethings

Printed in the USA
CPSIA information can be obtained
at www.ICGtesting.com
CBHW080847031224
18319CB00042B/1765